Three Steps in Defeating Temptation

Insights from James 4:7

Three Steps in Defeating Temptation

Three Steps in Defeating Temptation
Insights from James 4:7

By Lyle Dukes

All scripture quotations, unless otherwise noted, are from the Holy Bible, King James version.

ISBN 1-888918-04-7

Lyle and Deborah Dukes Ministries
P.O. Box 431
Woodbridge, Virginia 22194

Harvest Word Publishing, Inc.
P.O. Box 4514
Woodbridge, Virginia 22194

Printed in the United States of America

Cover Design By
Tamara Jones

Table of Contents

Acknowledgments

Functionality is not something that we are born with. Psalm 51:5 says, "Behold, I was shapen in iniquity, and in sin did my mother conceive me." Life in Christ is kind of a journey out of dysfunction and into the ways of God. I realize that if it had not been for functional models in my life, I would not be useful to the Kingdom. I want to thank our Lord Jesus Christ for His provision of these models. I want to thank all the teachers and counselors that have imparted to me over the years. You have all shared in the development of this manuscript. I want to especially thank my wife, Co-Pastor Deborah Dukes, who walked with me and gave me understanding as we weathered our storms together and taught me how to enjoy the sunshine of a brand new day.

To the wonderful and faithful team of editors Jim Gillis, Shenell Shepard, Christine Mallory, Nichelle Gardner, Lori Brooks and Tamara Jones, I thank you for your labor of love. To the Harvest Life Changers Church Family and Partners of Lyle and Deborah Dukes Ministries, thank you for your relationship, prayers and support.

Pastor Lyle Dukes

Preface

"This know also, that in the last days perilous times shall come.
2 *For men shall be lovers of their own selves, covetous, boasters,*
proud, blasphemers, disobedient to parents, unthankful, unholy,
3 *Without natural affection, trucebreakers, false accusers, inconti-*
nent, fierce, despisers of those that are good, 4 *Traitors, heady, high-*
minded, lovers of pleasures more than lovers of God; 5 *Having a*
form of godliness, but denying the power thereof: from such turn
away." II Timothy 3:1-5 [Emphasis added]

Guess what? "Perilous times" are here! This passage of scripture in II Timothy seems to describe the age in which we currently live with incredible accuracy. With all the things that we have to contend with we certainly need God's help. In a world that seems to become more evil by the day, there is a need for some explicit direction from God.

Just 50 years ago, the level of temptation was not nearly as intimidating, but the enemy has sent an onslaught of sinful activities for humankind, including Christians, to deal with. From an array of alcoholic beverages to the most potent of drugs (crack, heroin, etc.), addictive substances are as easy to access as going down to the corner store to buy groceries. Illicit sex, gambling, and homosexuality are no longer confined to the red light district of our major cities but can be accessed by our children right in the sanctity of our homes through the Internet and our televisions. Our schools have become less rule-oriented and more violent. Everywhere you look there is something sinful that is designed to appeal to your flesh. Strong temptation is everywhere.

> *"Blessed is the man that endureth temptation: for when he is tried, he shall receive the crown of life, which the Lord hath promised to them that love him."* James 1:12

This book is for anyone that has faced, is currently facing or will face strong temptation. When I speak of strong temptation, I am not talking about something that you can just give up or walk away from just because you choose to. I am talking about something that takes real power to overcome; a struggle with choices, not just something that you have, but something that has you. It is the kind of problem that causes you to face and fight a powerful desire within and when it is all over, although you have obtained the victory, you have lost something in the battle. You have left something behind.

I believe King David reflected upon strong temptation in his life in Psalm 40 when he said:

> *"I waited patiently for the LORD; and he inclined unto me, and heard my cry. 2 He brought me up also out of an horrible pit, out of the miry clay..."* [Emphasis added]

I was raised in the South in the early stages of my life and I can identify with "miry clay." It was different from just mud. Clay was thick and would grab onto you. If you ever had your foot stuck in this clay, getting it out was a task. When you finally got your foot out, sometimes your shoe would be left behind.

Strong temptation is like this clay; you have to fight to get free and sometimes you lose something in the process. You may have to lose years, friends, money, your reputation and relationships on the way to freedom, but whatever it takes, it is worth it to be free and right with God.

Strong temptation is difficult to deal with. Before it is all over, you may have cried more tears than you would have ever imagined. It may have worked on your last nerve or caused you to grapple with insurmountable levels of frustration. Dealing with strong temptation may have brought about almost overwhelming degrees of depression and caused you to work through the guilt and shame that invited you to attend copious pity parties. You may have experienced the disappointment and pain of relapse and battled doubt and unbelief with every fiber of your faith (while almost giving up over a thousand times); just remember, strong temptation is difficult, indeed.

This book deals with real people, real problems, real temptations and most importantly, a real process for REAL VICTORY.

> *"There hath no temptation taken you but such as is common to man: but God is faithful, who will not suffer you to be tempted above that ye are able; but will with the temptation also make a* <u>*way to escape*</u>*, that ye may be able to bear it."* I Corinthians 10:13 [Emphasis added]

The main objective of this book is to examine and present the biblical process of overcoming temptation. Please remain prayerfully focused as we deal with the three steps found in James 4:7 concerning the defeat of temptation:

> *"Submit yourselves therefore to God. Resist the devil, and he will flee from you."*

These steps are (1) submitting yourself to God, (2) putting up a strong resistance and (3) letting the devil (and temptation) flee from you.

Foreword

Many times when we talk about the struggles of a Christian, we remain pretty generic. It is so easy to escape the challenges and details of the temptation battle by saying things like "Jesus is the answer" or "God will see you through." Most of us have paraded these "surface" slogans because we did not know anything beyond them, and if the truth be told, a slogan will not get you any victories. We knew the "what," but we just never knew the "how." "How is Jesus the answer?" "How will God see me through?" "How will God make a way for me?"

The Bible declares you shall know the truth and the truth will make you free.[1] To "know" means to become intimate with. In other words, you shall become intimate with the truth and the truth will make you free. God gives answers, solutions, instructions and guidance through His Word! The Word of God addresses real issues through its powerful and anointed presentation that will destroy yokes today as it did centuries ago.

As we begin to look into the Word of God, we will find the right antidote to be successful against any temptation. Jesus Christ declared, "I am the way, the truth and the life."[2] If we want to find our way out of temptation, we must first find Jesus for He is the way. When you find Jesus, you find power and promise. He further stated that if we want to travel His auspicious and victorious path, we must deny ourselves, take up our cross and follow Him.[3] I believe that by following Jesus, through His Word, we can escape any temptation

[1] St. John 8:32 And ye shall know the truth, and the truth shall make you free.
[2] St. John 14:6 Jesus saith unto him, I am the way, the truth, and the life: no man cometh unto the Father, but by me.
[3] St. Matthew 16:24 Then said Jesus unto his disciples, if any man will come after me, let him deny himself, and take up his cross, and follow me.

that the enemy uses to try to destroy us. The scripture declares in I Corinthians 10:13:

> *"There hath no temptation taken you but such as is common to man: but God is faithful, who will not suffer you to be tempted above that ye are able; but will with the temptation also make a way to escape, that you may be able to bear it."*

Aren't you glad that God is faithful? He provides just what is needed for our present struggle. Temptations are real. This is why it is necessary to address this subject matter. It is something every Christian will face. Even Jesus Christ had to deal with temptation.[4]

Hebrews 4:15 states:

> *"For we have not an high priest which cannot be touched with the feeling of our infirmities; but was in all points tempted like as we are, yet without sin."*

If you want to beat temptation, follow the One who has already championed the cause. Jesus never fails.

[4] St. Matthew, Chapter 4

STEP I

SUBMIT YOURSELF TO GOD

"Submit yourselves therefore to God..." James 4:7

Chapter One

Yield to God

"Now be ye not stiffnecked, as your fathers were, but yield yourselves unto the LORD and enter into his sanctuary..." II Chronicles 30:8[5]

If you are going to have any real victory over temptation it is imperative that you yield to God. If you ever hope to see a pattern of success against the copious evil enticements that you endure, you must posture yourself correctly.

Temptation is no joke. It is a very serious matter. Since it is so serious, we need to insure it receives its proper level of attention. Many tragic failures have resulted from what appeared to be minor temptations. Temptation is the door that leads to destruction. If we can "close" the door of temptation, then families, businesses, relationships, and finances can be preserved. Perhaps, if we can "close" the door of temptation, nations will survive.

Temptation is a force of evil that deals specifically with the carnal or sinful nature of mankind with the mission of disrupting godly, wholesome and positive patterns. It is a powerful enticement to lure individuals to commit illegal, immoral or unwise acts. Temptation uses the potent inducements of pleasure, promise and sat-

[5] II Chronicles 30:8 Now be ye not stiffnecked, as your fathers were, but yield yourselves unto the LORD, and enter into his sanctuary, which he hath sanctified for ever: and serve the LORD your God, that the fierceness of his wrath may turn away from you.

isfaction to bait people, while carefully concealing the consequences of loss and destruction. It is a powerful tool the enemy uses in his effort to obliterate the human race. The devil has to start someplace and one of his favorite starting places is temptation. Since temptation is such a powerful force, you need power to defeat it. The only proven method of defeating temptation is to have God on your side. Jesus said in St. Luke 10:19

> *"Behold, I give unto you power to tread on serpents and scorpions, and over all the power of the enemy: and nothing shall by any means hurt you."* [Emphasis added]

What a powerful thing to know! This power is not just something that you need on an "on call" basis or "every now and then"; you need this power one hundred percent of the time. You need a resident power from God. The reason you need a resident power is that temptation will knock on your door every day. The truth be known, all human beings must deal with temptation on a daily basis. Since we know this to be the case, daily submission to God is prolifically in order.

Submitting to God means yielding everything about yourself to His Will and plan for your life. Every care, problem, situation and circumstance, give it all to God. If He is going to "cover" us, we must give it all to Him.

When a person gets into a car accident one of the first questions that is asked is "Are you covered by insurance?" Depending on the policy, that person will have to pay or have the insurance pay the costs. If the person only has collision insurance, then not all damages will be paid for. God wants us to yield our all to Him: our minds, hearts, bodies and souls. Get it all under the coverage of God.

The Power of Repentance

Getting under the "coverage" of God starts with repentance. To repent means to ask God for forgiveness of our sins, transgressions, and all wrongdoings against Him and His Will. This request to God must come from the heart and must be accompanied by a sincere degree of contrition. It is not just repeating some words that you read in a book—but it is being real with God concerning all that you are. Repenting is laying your whole life before Him with all of its flaws, failures and foolishness. It is interesting that the longer you live for Christ, the more sensitive to Him you become. Therefore, repentance becomes a common element in the life of a mature Christian.

Repentance is the basic component that gets us past the walls of separation caused by sin and into the presence of the Lord. Acts 3:19 states,

> *"Repent ye therefore and be converted, that your sins may be blotted out, when the times of refreshing shall come forth from the presence of the LORD;"*

Repentance is the "front door" of yielding to God. Going through this door means turning from your ways, life style and patterns of the past. You must forsake your agenda and adopt His. This process places you in a posture of yielding to God. Remember, if you are yielded to God you can defeat temptation. Real yielding cannot occur without repentance.

When true repentance is displayed, many tremendous things are initiated. Repentance places you in a position of humility, which allows you to hear and receive instructions from God. In order to navigate successfully through a tempting and flesh-fulfilling environment, it is imperative that we hear from God. He will tell us what

[6] Psalm 46:1 God is our refuge and strength, a very present help in trouble.

we need to know during the time of temptation. Psalm 46:1 states that He is "...a very present help in trouble."[6]

Repentance also helps to cleanse our spirit. When we confess and repent for our sins, we are actually changing the spiritual landscape that resides within. The Power of God is ushered in to wash us from the inside out. I John 1:9-10 states,

> *"If we confess our sins, he is faithful and just to forgive us our sins, and to cleanse us from all unrighteousness.*
> 10 *If we say that we have not sinned, we make him a liar, and His word is not in us."*

Repentance is yielding to God by releasing the old and trusting God for the new.

Maintaining a Posture of Humility

Submitting or yielding to God is not a short term or one time event. It is something that you as a believer must do perpetually if you are going to be successful in overcoming temptation. The more that you are yielded to God, the more successful you will be in dealing with temptation. Notice, you are less likely to sin or fall under the "spell" of temptation when you have just come out of a good worship service. This is because your spirit has yielded to God. You are "positionally" stronger in God because your mind, heart and soul have been saturated in His presence.

So, how do you maintain this powerful positioning throughout the week? The key is humility. Humility pushes the flesh down and allows the Holy Spirit to reign. Humility keeps you reaching for what God wants. As you go throughout your day, humility helps to keep you hungry for God. St. Matthew 5:6 states,

[7] St. Matthew 26:39 And he went a little farther, and fell on his face, and prayed, saying, O my Father, if it be possible, let this cup pass from me: nevertheless not as I will, but as thou wilt.

> *"Blessed are they which do hunger and thirst after righteousness: for they shall be filled."*

A humble spirit says what Jesus said in the Garden of Gethsemane, "…not as I will, but as thou wilt."[7] A humble spirit keeps you praying and looking for directions from God for the next step. "The steps of a good man are ordered by the LORD…"[8]

A pattern of humility, over time, will break you free from the desire for present temptations. If you keep trusting God and submitting every aspect of your life to Him, including your struggles, feelings, pains and insecurities, He will promote you to a new level—a level where the things that used to tempt or bother you no longer have any effect. I Peter 5:6 says,

> *"Humble yourselves therefore under the mighty hand of God, that he may exalt you in due time:"*

Humility says, "God, I am totally trusting You and Your process!"

[8] Psalm 37:23 The steps of a good man are ordered by the LORD: and he delighteth in his way.

Chapter Two

Become A Worshipper

"For we are the circumcision, which worship God in the spirit, and rejoice in Christ Jesus, and have no confidence in the flesh." Philippians 3:3

Becoming a worshipper is placing a consistent and perpetual focus on the Lord Jesus through our worship and is one of the most important ways to beat temptation. One of the most vital tools to combat temptation is spiritual focus, which is imperative for the believer to obtain victory. Worshippers have a spiritual focus that supplies the stamina needed for spiritual warfare.

Gaining a greater level of intimacy with God places you in a posture of strength so that when temptation arises you can overcome it. Where does temptation find you? Will it find you in a posture of weakness or strength? Worshippers have power because they are in a close relationship with God. Since He is close, there is the unique ability to access His power. God wants us to be victorious so we need to become worshippers.

Becoming a worshipper takes time. Some time needs to be logged in around the "altar." There needs to be communication with

God to the point that familiarity turns into intimacy. As you spend time in the presence of the Lord, a transformation will occur. God gives "special downloads" to worshippers. If we are going to beat temptation, we must be worshippers because worshippers beat temptation. In the Bible, Joseph was successful in beating lust in the incident with Potiphar's wife because he was a worshipper. At various stages of his life, the scripture says that God was with Joseph because he was a worshipper.[9]

Daniel was a worshipper. Although challenged by his peers, he continued to worship God. In fact, he opened up the windows of his dwelling and prayed openly. When Daniel was sentenced to the lions' den, he could only look to God in his situation because he was a worshipper. God was there and gave him deliverance. Daniel could beat the fear of the lions' den and those who tried to intimidate him because he had spent time with God. There is a power that a worshipper possesses and this power is obtained because of a relationship with God.

Spiritual activity is the lifeblood of your worship—it keeps your worship alive. Guard your spiritual activity by going to church, praying, fasting, giving, working in ministry, and studying the Word. Like faith without works is dead, worship without sacrifice is dead also. The level of worship needed to beat temptation will directly correspond with how close you have become to God. Worship brings you into His presence and at His feet.

You Can Beat Temptation Through Your Worship

Worshippers tend to be ready when temptation arrives unannounced or unexpected, because they have a resident power. This resident power comes because they are incessantly and perpetually in the presence of God. A worshipper, by his very nature, stays at the

[9] Genesis 39:2 And the LORD was with Joseph, and he was a prosperous man; and he was in the house of his master the Egyptian.

throne of God and connected to the Will of God. Worship is not confined to the church building. Worshippers are walking in the presence of God and therefore "connected" to God. No matter where they are, they are always looking for God in every situation. The scripture says in Psalm 46:1,

> *"God is our refuge and strength, a very present help in trouble."*

Since worshippers also continually place themselves in the presence of God, it is hard for the devil to do anything because the Father is around. It is important to maintain your posture of worship because the power of a worshipper is connection to his God.

Worship is important if you are going to defeat temptation. It is so important that the worshipper continue to maintain his labor of love for God. You must keep looking up, looking out and looking for the blessings of God in your life. Your intimate relationship with God, through your worship, will defeat temptation.

Chapter Three

Make Up Your Mind

"Let this mind be in you, which was also in Christ Jesus:"
Philippians 2:5

In order to defeat temptation, it is important to have a made up mind. Submitting yourself to God has all to do with making up your mind. Your mind houses your thoughts and your thoughts dictate your actions. Your actions establish your footing concerning the Will of God. When you make up your mind, you are actually stabilizing yourself in God. Making up your mind means being steadfast concerning the Will of God. It is espousing His will and plan for your life by releasing your mindset and adopting His ways. It is important to have a made up mind. The devil can defeat us when we do not. Philippians 2:5 says,

> *"Let this mind be in you which was also in Christ Jesus:"*

Adam and Eve suffered because they did not have a made up mind. They lost out on what God had for them because they wavered in their commitment to God. They were beguiled by the serpent. In

Genesis 3:3 God said, "Ye shall not eat of it, neither shall ye touch it, lest ye die."[10] The serpent used one word to trick her by saying, "Ye shall not surely die."[11] Because they did not have a made up mind, they allowed their minds to be changed concerning what God had said. When you have a made up mind, it is difficult for the enemy to do anything to you. The Bible says in Proverbs 23:7, "For as he thinketh in his heart, so is he."[12] Everything that you think has something to do with who you are.

A made up mind has a clear direction. It is fortified by an uncompromising, steadfast belief in God. Its dialogue states, "I am standing on the Word of God. I am following Jesus. I am sold out for Christ." When you have a made up mind, it is difficult for anything to interrupt your current schedule that God has laid out before you. The devil has trouble tempting people who have a made up mind. They are more stable in their spiritual walk.

James 1:8 says,

"A double minded man is unstable in all his ways."

When James talks about being double minded, he is speaking about moving from one thought to another; about oscillating or vacillating between what is right and what is wrong. When your mind is made up to serve God, the enemy has trouble dealing with defeating you concerning your purpose.

Jesus was a great example. His mind was made up and He relied on the Word of God. After each temptation in St. Matthew 4, He told the devil emphatically that he submitted himself to God's Word. After each temptation He said: "It is written…" Let's look at how Jesus responded to the devil in St. Matthew, Chapter 4:

[10] Genesis 3:3 But of the fruit of the tree which is in the midst of the garden, God hath said, Ye shall not eat of it, neither shall ye touch it, lest ye die.
[11] Genesis 3:4 And the serpent said unto the woman, Ye shall not surely die:
[12] Proverbs 23:7 For as he thinketh in his heart, so is he: Eat and drink, saith he to thee; but his heart is not with thee.

> *"It is written, Man shall not live by bread alone, but by every word that proceedeth out of the mouth of God."*[13]
>
> *"It is written again, Thou shall not tempt the Lord thy God."*[14]
>
> *"Get thee hence, Satan: for it is written, Thou shall worship the Lord thy God, and him only shalt thou serve."*[15]

This indicates that Jesus had His mind made up and thus He became a living example for believers to follow. The example He set shows us that we must stand on God's Word. We should not doubt or succumb to unbelief.

[13] St. Matthew 4:4
[14] St. Matthew 4:7
[15] St. Matthew 4:10

Chapter Four

Be Obedient to God's Word

"Ye did run well; who did hinder you that ye should not obey the truth?" Galatians 5:7

Obedience is the power to submit to God's Will and enforce it in your life. It is impossible to submit yourself to God without being obedient to His Word. It is important for you to rely on the Word of God as your instruction manual. It will enable you to be victorious at every turn. The Bible says the Word of God is a "lamp unto our feet, a light unto our path."[16] It shows you where to go and how to be victorious. As a lamp and a light are for a traveler, the Word of God lights our pathway. It shows obstacles which could become stumbling blocks and helps to navigate beyond those obstacles. This is necessary for being victorious at the time of temptation. It is important for you to believe and to trust God's Word. Sometimes it seems that you know the right answer. But align yourself with the Word because God always has the right answer.

Many times we hear the Word of God but we do not follow through with what it asks of us. Obedience means not only hearing, but also keeping the Word of God. Luke 8:12-13 says:

"Those by the way side are they that hear; then cometh

[16] Psalm 119:105 Thy word is a lamp unto my feet, and a light unto my path.

the devil, and taketh away the word out of their hearts, lest they should believe and be saved. 13 *They on the rock are they, which, when they hear, receive the word with joy; and these have no root, which for a while believe, and in time of temptation fall away."*

Victory has all to do with you continually, incessantly and perpetually believing God's Word. An established pattern of walking with God means trusting His Word through experience, trials, storms and situations. It means believing God in the face of temptation. Revelation 3:10 says:

> *"Because thou hast kept the word of my patience, I also will keep thee from the hour of temptation, which shall come upon all the world, to try them that dwell upon the earth."*

Keeping God's Word will give you certain victory in the hour of temptation. I John 2:5 says:

> *"But whoso keepeth his word, in him verily is the love of God perfected: hereby know we that we are in him."*

God wants us to understand the power of His Word, but the power of His Word cannot come to pass without obedience.

Obedience is absolutely imperative to win the battles of a successful campaign. To prevail, each soldier has to be connected to the overall strategy by something called orders. If there are no orders for each military unit, then there is a greater opportunity for defeat. First, there is the opportunity to be defeated by the enemy who is seeking to destroy us. The Word of God says the devil goes about seeking whom he may devour.[17] Secondly, there is defeat by "friend-

[17] I Peter 5:8 Be sober, be vigilant; because your adversary the devil, as a roaring lion, walketh about, seeking whom he may devour;

ly fire." Friendly fire is an attack that is not coming from the enemy, but from your own camp! Sometimes we destroy ourselves because we are not walking in the Word of God or "under orders."

It is important to be obedient to the Word of God because it will give us triumph. Being obedient to the Word of God is not as easy as it sounds. It appears simple, but sometimes it is very difficult because the Word of God deals with truth. Truth is not the easiest thing to deal with. In order to be successful, we must deal with truth. The scripture says you must "know the truth and the truth shall make you free."[18] Truth causes us to deal with ourselves and places us in a posture to defeat temptation.

Hebrews 4:12 says:

> *"For the word of God is quick, and powerful, and sharper than any twoedged sword, piercing even to the dividing asunder of soul and spirit, and of the joints and marrow, and is a discerner of the thoughts and intents of the heart."* [Emphasis added]

The Word of God reaches areas that we do not wish to deal with. Lust, greed, pride, other vices, and insecurities are areas where the enemy will try to tempt you. The truth of the Word of God slips into your cognitive mind and scrutinizes your actions. God wants to develop Christians that rely on His Word.

Defeating temptation has all to do with being obedient to God's Word. In His Word is the truth to deal with each temptation that we have to face. Freedom comes by way of the truth of God. When we are not obedient to God, we become open to all kinds of temptation. The door swings open for the enemy and his demonic forces to deal with us and then we suffer the consequences of the judgment of the Word of God, which is the wrath of God. It is vital-

[18] St. John 8:32 And ye shall know the truth, and the truth shall make you free.

ly important for us to close the door of temptation with the Word so that we can be successful in our walk with Christ.

Chapter Five

Surround Yourself with Godliness

"...godliness is profitable unto all things, having promise of the life that now is, and of that which is to come." I Timothy 4:8

One of the major elements of being successful is posturing yourself in an environment that is conducive to spiritual growth. It is imperative for those that want to defeat temptation to be in a state to overcome the enemy.

The Bible says in I Timothy 6:6:

> *"But godliness with contentment is great gain."*

There is a powerful anointing that comes upon those that trust God's process and are positioned in His plan. There are so many Christians that are defeated just because of their environment. The scripture says in II Timothy 3:5:

> *"Having a form of godliness, but denying the power thereof: from such turn away."*

It tells us this because there are some people that portray a godly way. They may come to church and may carry a Bible, however, they are not rooted in God's process because of their environment. The scripture says in I Corinthians 15:33:

> *"Be not deceived: evil communications corrupt good manners."*

Sometimes the people you hang around will cause you to lose out on your spiritual anointing. They may sap your spiritual strength and cause you to go down the wrong path. In order to be successful, you have to submit yourself to God. Submitting yourself to God simply means connecting with the people and things God has placed in your environment for your spiritual edification.

In II Corinthians 6:14,

> *"Be ye not unequally yoked together with unbelievers: for what fellowship hath righteousness with unrighteousness? and what communion hath light with darkness?"*

It is possible to be "in church" (church member), yet not in the right environment while out of the church building. Under these circumstances, the Word of God is negated because you are in the wrong place at the wrong time. When God gives you a Word, He gives you an environment to live and walk in that Word. If we have the wrong people on board or find ourselves in the wrong places, then we go against the "grain" of the plan God has for our lives. We need to surround ourselves with godliness. That means being spiritually discerning regarding everything about your environment: your thoughts, your friends, the places you go and the things that you do.

Acts 2:42 states:

> *"And they continued stedfastly in the apostles' doctrine and fellowship, and in breaking of bread, and in prayers."*

These saints of God in the Book of Acts were successful because they continued in the plan that God had laid out for them. They were steadfast in the Word and in fellowship. They were around the right people and in the right environment for growth. If you want something to grow, you must have the right environment. You may have a good seed but if you do not have good soil, the plant will never grow. Surrounding yourself with godliness means submitting yourself to God by planting yourself in the environment that He has established for you to be successful in.

Philippians 4:8 says:

> *"Finally, brethren, whatsoever things are true, whatsoever things are honest, whatsoever things are just, whatsoever things are pure, whatsoever things are lovely, whatsoever things are of good report; if there be any virtue, and if there by any praise, think on these things."*

If we are going to be triumphant and overcome temptation, we must ensure that we are operating in the place and in the posture God has laid out for us. It is important for us to become rooted and grounded in God's Word, His Will and His Way. When we do this and temptation comes, we will be strengthened to quench the fiery darts that the enemy throws our way.

STEP II

PUT UP A STRONG RESISTANCE AGAINST THE DEVIL AND HIS TEMPTATION

"...Resist the devil..." James 4:7

Chapter Six

Do Not Dialogue With the Devil

"And the serpent said unto the woman, Ye shall not surely die:" Genesis 3:4

As challenging as it is to get through the first step, submitting yourself to God, the real battle begins during this second step. It is here that everything in step one is put to the test. Have you really yielded to God? Is your worship as strong as it needs to be? Have you really made up your mind to serve God? Are you emphatically obedient to God's Word? Have you surrounded yourself with godliness? These questions will be answered on the proving ground of challenge.

The devil wants no more than to take you out and destroy your life. He has a whole arsenal of fiery armaments that he plans to throw at you. God tells us in His Word that He has given us what we need to be successful if we can believe. Ephesians 6:16 states,

> *"Above all, taking the shield of faith, wherewith ye shall be able to quench all the fiery darts of the wicked."*

One of the ways that the devil attacks is through something I call "negative spiritual dialogue." He hits you with temptation when you entertain what appear to be innocent thoughts. Through this dialogue, the enemy plants evil thoughts as seeds of destruction.

This negative spiritual dialogue all happens within the framework of your mind. It catches you in the middle of regular thought processing, something that you do several times a minute every day of your life. Your mind is always involved in dialogue whether verbally with a person or non-verbally with yourself ("What do I want to eat today?" etc.), and while you are sleeping, through dreams. There is an ongoing conversation that is accompanied by a great deal of thought analysis. The enemy merely joins in the "chat."

The devil tries to slip into your thought patterns early in the game, before you have made up your mind concerning right and wrong. He hopes to reach you before your belief is consummated concerning the Word of God. While conversing with your mind, the adversary peddles his deception, doubt and disbelief. He sells us on shortcuts, schemes and lies as well as the short-term pleasures or benefits of doing wrong. The enemy never allows us to see the judgment and bondage that sin will eventually bring.

This enticement is solely based upon our willingness to ponder or contemplate the <u>idea</u> of beneficial wrongdoing and pleasurable sin. If you are "sold out" to what is right, then negative spiritual dialogue cannot occur. However, if you are open to entertain these ideas, and allow negative spiritual dialogue, as Eve did in the Garden of Eden, then lust is conceived in your heart and you have started down the road of destruction.

James 1:14-16 tells us,

> *"...every man is tempted, when he is drawn away of his own lust, and enticed.* 15 *Then when lust hath conceived, it bringeth forth sin: and sin, when it is finished, bringeth forth death.* 16 *Do not err, my beloved brethren."*

Whatever you do, make sure that you do not dialogue with the devil. Put in place a "zero tolerance" policy. Examine your ways, actions and thought patterns and whenever the devil tries to put in his two cents, reject it. Do not entertain it. It is more deadly than it looks. Ephesians 4:27 states,

> *"Neither give place to the devil."*

Very good advice! Protect yourself from destruction. Guard your internal and external conversation. Ephesians 4:22-24 says,

> *"...put off concerning the former conversation the old man, which is corrupt according to the deceitful lusts;*
> 23 *And be renewed in the spirit of your mind;* 24 *And that ye put on the new man, which after God is created in righteousness and true holiness."*

Remember, do not dialogue with the devil.

Chapter Seven

Stop Living on the Verge of Sin

"Watch ye and pray, lest ye enter into temptation. The spirit truly is ready, but the flesh is weak." Mark 14:38

Your ability to put up a strong resistance against the devil and his temptations has much to do with your personal disposition. Some individuals will not experience victory over temptation because they cannot commit to changing their past patterns. They honestly desire to accept Jesus Christ as their Savior but for whatever reason, will not leave their faulty and sinful practices and remove themselves from their wicked and defective environment. They just continue on, living on the verge of sin.

In Genesis, Chapter 4, when Cain had given the wrong offering, God gave him the opportunity to get it straight. Notice that Cain had a mind to worship and sacrifice to God, but he never corrected his faulty manner. Look at what God told Cain:

> *"If thou doest well, shalt thou not be accepted? and if thou doest not well, sin lieth at the door...."* Genesis 4:7

Basically, God was telling Cain, "if you keep operating like this, pretty soon you are going to fall into sin." That is just what he did—he killed his brother Abel. If you work around mud, pretty soon you are going to get some on you. Hebrews 12:1 tells us to,

> *"...lay aside every weight, and the sin which doth so easily beset us, and let us run with patience the race that is set before us,..."*

In other words, give up the corrupt, harmful and vile activities of your past and then run! Move quickly away from the place of past performance. Do not go back, think back or even look back. As long as you remain disobedient and hang around that thing you will soon be back in sin. You are making the devil's job too easy.

Stop getting into situations that you know will mess you up. Stop going to places that you know will sap your spiritual strength. Do not even entertain the very thought of it. If you think back, you will go back. If you never really removed yourself from that set of circumstances, the journey back will be a quick one. If you are an alcoholic, remove all the beer from your refrigerator and pour it out. If you used to be a smoker, throw away that secret stash and please do not sit in the smoking section. If you had a lust problem, stay off the porn sites on the Internet. Do not get on the computer at all if you cannot control yourself.

If you are going to be victorious, you must get out of Sodom [Read Genesis Chapter 19] before the city burns with you in it. Jesus says,

> *"Watch ye and pray, lest ye enter into temptation. The spirit truly is ready; but the flesh is weak."*
> St. Mark 14:38

Since you know the flesh is weak, you must make a commitment to keep yourself in an environment that is conducive to spirituality. Stop living on the verge of sin.

"Good understanding giveth favour: but the way of transgressors is hard." Proverbs 13:15

"Righteousness keepeth him that is upright in the way: but wickedness overthroweth the sinner." Proverbs 13:6

Chapter Eight

Place No Confidence in the Flesh

"For we are the circumcision, which worship God in the Spirit, and rejoice in Christ Jesus, and have no confidence in the flesh." Philippians 3:3

You must gain a better perspective of what a challenge it is to develop a strong resistance against the devil and his temptations. Without a good understanding of the frailties of the flesh, you are susceptible to fall victim to temptation by a "false reality" of your personal strength.

The fact is, the flesh is very weak. If you allow it to operate on its own, it will eventually fall prey to temptation. Again, Jesus emphasized for us to:

> *"Watch and pray, that ye enter not into temptation: the spirit indeed is willing, but the flesh is weak."*
> St. Matthew 26:41

There must be a concerted effort on the part of every Christian to keep the flesh from succumbing to temptation and entering into sin. You need to be covered by the blood of Jesus, obedient to the Word of God, and led by the wonderful guidance of the Holy Spirit to keep yourself from falling. You must be very serious concerning what you are up against, and scrutinize every thought and idea that comes to your mind. Prayer and supplication along with fasting will help you to maintain your spiritual stability.

This plethora of spiritual activity is mentioned because many of us do not recognize how unstable and powerless the flesh actually is. The enemy wants to dupe us into believing that we do not need any help. If we do not seek help, we are worse than a sitting duck. The anointed Apostle Paul stated in Romans 7:18:

> *"For I know that in me (that is, in my flesh,) dwelleth no good thing:..."*

It is going to take all the spiritual strength that you can muster to beat temptation. If you have not been tempted like this, prepare yourself, it's coming your way. When temptation comes, meet it at the gate of your mind and whatever you do, don't entertain it. If temptation ever gets an inch, you can believe it will take a mile.

One of the great dangers for the people of God is complacency. There is something that happens to people that have been "in church" for a while. They have the propensity to drop their guard as apathy and indifference settle in. You have seen it; people work in the service of the Lord for years and then all of a sudden they fall in a terrible sin or just drop out of sight. Somewhere down the line they forgot that they were living in a war zone. In this combat environment, you need all the God you can get!

> *"...be strong in the Lord, and in the power of his might.*
> 11 *Put on the whole armour of God, that ye may be able to stand against the wiles of the devil.* 12 *For we wrestle not against flesh and blood, but against principalities, against powers, against the rulers of the darkness of this world, against spiritual wickedness in high places."*
> Ephesians 6:10-12

You need to recognize that the flesh cannot make it on its own. Since it cannot be victorious, the flesh needs to be willfully placed under the subjection of the Holy Spirit. Paul told the Corinthian Church,

> *"But I keep under my body, and bring it into subjection: lest that by any means, when I have preached to others, I myself should be a castaway."* I Corinthians 9:27

The emotions, feelings and desires of the flesh need to function under the auspices of internal spiritual leadership. II Corinthians 10:3-4 states,

> *"For though we walk in the flesh, we do not war after the flesh:* 4 *For the weapons of our warfare are not carnal, but mighty* <u>*through*</u> *God to the pulling down of strongholds;"* [Emphasis added]

It is going to take embracing God by faith in the totality of who He is for you to successfully overcome strong temptation. As you resist the devil, learn how to rely on God's direction. Romans 8.3 states,

> *"For what the law could not do, in that it was weak through the flesh, God sending his own Son in the likeness of sinful flesh, and for sin, condemned sin in the flesh:..."*

So, you can obtain a resounding victory over temptation even with weakness of the flesh. However, you must be committed to reject the mannerisms and customs of the flesh. Rejection of this kind can only be done effectively, time and time again, through the power of Jesus Christ.

Chapter Nine

Fight the Feeling

"For we have not an high priest which cannot be touched with the feeling of our infirmities; but was in all points tempted like as we are, yet without sin." Hebrews 4:15

Up to this point in our discussion of the second step, we addressed the fine details of how to conduct ourselves during times of temptation. We looked at how not to dialogue with the devil, how to stop living a haphazard life, how to stop living on the verge of sin, and how to view our flesh in terms of temptation and sin.

In this chapter, emphasis is placed on the elements of battle. It is important to examine the essence of what the challenge of temptation will bring. In other words, you need to lock down on the fact that there is going to be a battle. It will not be just a fight, but it will be a knock down, drag-out-fight. The word "resist", in and of itself, entails that there is going to be some kind of struggle. Resistance deals with going against the grain. If we are going to resist the devil, this means that we are going against the devil and all of the forces of darkness. However, we do not have to be dismayed or intimidated because the Word of God promises us that we will have victory. II Peter 1:4 says,

"Whereby are given unto us exceeding great and pre-

> *cious promises: that by these ye might be partakers of the divine nature, having escaped the corruption that is in the world through lust."*

So, we can be victorious even though we face a fight. We must not let our feelings get the best of us. We must continue to live beyond our feelings. Do not allow your desires to overtake you. Never give in to things like loneliness, depression, oppression, fear or insecurities. If you let your feelings drive you, you will lose control of your destiny. It would be unrealistic and inhuman to say that you should not have these feelings—you will, however, do not let them dictate your thoughts and actions. As human beings, we are susceptible to different emotions and will face challenges that speak to some intrinsic, life changing fears and dilemmas. Nevertheless, we must maintain a spiritual focus so that we do not lose our purpose and plan that God has given us. The devil desires to take us out of the plan of God. He does this by tempting us and hoping to get into our feelings and emotions so they will drive us into areas God did not plan for our lives, and into directions God does not wish us to go.

James 1:14 says,

> *"But every man is tempted, when he is drawn away of his own lust, and enticed."*

You must fight to stay in control. As noted earlier, the Apostle Paul recognized that he had to bring his body under subjection. We must do the same. There is going to be a battle. If you want to be free, understand that freedom has a price. If you want to be emancipated from your present bondage, there is a struggle that you must endure. If you are going to have the yokes broken from your life, then there is going to be some pain that you must overcome. What you must understand is there will be a fight. In the fight, give it all you have. Make sure you do not let the enemy and your feelings take control of your mind. You must gain spiritual superiority. If you keep your mind, then you can be successful. As mentioned earlier, the scripture tells us,

> *"For we wrestle not against flesh and blood, but against principalities, against powers, against the rulers of the darkness of this world, against spiritual wickedness in high places."* Ephesians 6:12

If we are going to be in a fight, we must be equipped for battle. The scripture says in Ephesians 6:13-17,

> *"Wherefore take unto you the whole armour of God, that*
> *ye may be able to withstand in the evil day, and having*
> *done all, to stand.* 14 *Stand therefore, having your loins*
> *girt about with truth, and having on the breastplate of*
> *righteousness;* 15 *And your feet shod with the prepara-*
> *tion of the gospel of peace;* 16 *Above all, taking the*
> *shield of faith, wherewith ye shall be able to quench all*
> *the fiery darts of the wicked.* 17 *And take the helmet of*
> *salvation, and the sword of the Spirit, which is the word*
> *of God:"*

As we don the spiritual equipment that God has given us, we can be successful. First and foremost, beating temptation means that you must have your loins girded with truth. You must deal with the truth of your infractions, infirmities and weaknesses. You must have the breastplate of righteousness on which simply means you must walk upright before the Lord even in the heat of battle. We need our feet shod with the preparation of the gospel of peace. We need the Word of God to help us walk and find peace in the midst of the storm and in the midst of a warlike atmosphere. We need the shield of faith to be able to quench all of the weapons and all of the projectiles that the enemy will throw at us. We need something to stop the infiltration of his wicked devices. The shield of faith is your belief taking a stand for God. The enemy will challenge our very belief structure through temptation.

We also must have the sword of the Spirit, which is the Word of God. It is so important to have the Word of God in your life because while you are in the heat of the battle, while the bombs are flying, you need some orders on what to do. The Bible states that the Holy Spirit will bring back the Word of God to our remembrance.[19] This is why we need the sword of the Spirit. The sword acts as an offensive weapon, which causes us to fight whatever advances the enemy makes towards us.

Remember to keep fighting. Keep believing and give it all you've got. Strong temptation is not an easy thing to overcome. If you fight, however, God will grant you the victory. He stated in Isaiah 54:17,

> *"No weapon that is formed against thee shall prosper;..."*

In I Timothy 6:12 we find,

> *"Fight the good fight of faith, lay hold on eternal life, whereunto thou art also called, and hast professed a good profession before many witnesses."*

You must fight to stay in control. You must fight to stay right.

[19] St. John 14:26 But the Comforter, which is the Holy Ghost, whom the Father will send in my name, he shall teach you all things, and bring all things to your remembrance, whatsoever I have said unto you.

Chapter Ten

Don't Allow Yourself to Wander

"Be sober, be vigilant; because your adversary the devil, as a roaring lion, walketh about, seeking whom he may devour:" I Peter 5:8

The discussion in this section has been centered on resisting the devil in an overt manner. Now, I want to devote time to the danger of wandering or losing focus. It is so important to maintain our spiritual equanimity in God for us to be victorious. Maintaining our vision and purpose helps us to become stable in our walk with God. If we are stable, we have a better chance at defeating temptation when it comes our way.

Many times we lose our focus by looking at peripheral things rather than keeping our mind and attention on the main things. We major in minors and minor in majors. We become spiritual nomads and wander outside of our element, and God's Will. When we are outside of where God wants us to be we are vulnerable. It is then easier for the enemy to defeat us through temptation and the enticement of sin. Many times this happens after we have done something very good: attended a good service, experienced a great ministry accomplishment, or helped someone do something significant. We tend to become complacent and lethargic concerning our purpose and our destiny. We have the tendency to think that since we have accomplished one thing, that we can take our ease in Zion. This usually happens after we have a victory in a hard fought battle. But after the battle is over, it is not time to put up the weapons because the war continues. When you relax, even for a few seconds, the enemy will attack. In fact, he is looking for all of us to let down our guard. I Thessalonians 5:6-8 says,

> *"Therefore let us not sleep, as do others; but let us watch and be sober.* 7 *For they that sleep sleep in the night; and they that be drunken are drunken in the night.* 8 *But let us, who are of the day, be sober, putting on the breast-plate of faith and love; and for an helmet, the hope of salvation."*

Someone who is sober minded clearly knows where he or she is going. The opposite of being sober minded is being drunk. A drunken person has a fuzzy outlook, often stumbling and falling. In many instances they will end up where they did not want to go. God calls us to be sober. That means we have a specific direction and purpose; therefore not wandering. God is calling us to a new dimension and a new level. If we are going to embrace this new level, we must maintain our focus. We cannot allow ourselves to wander. Ephesians 5:15-17 says,

> *"See then that ye walk circumspectly, not as fools, but as wise,* 16 *Redeeming the time, because they days are evil.*
> 17 *Wherefore be ye not unwise, but understanding what the will of the Lord is."*

It is so important that we know where we are going. If we know where we are going spiritually, it is hard for the devil to knock us off track. He is hoping to find weak, helpless, feeble and impotent Christians. If he finds us in that state, we are easily devoured.

> *"Be sober, be vigilant; because your adversary the devil, as a roaring lion, walketh about, seeking whom he may*

devour:" I Peter 5:8

Have you ever found yourself in a situation and you don't know how you got there? Somewhere down the line we started to wander. Drifting is a terrible thing. Many people who fish know that drifting happens very subtly. Before you know it, you have floated several hundred yards without noticing. This can happen to us spiritually as well. The devil is banking on the fact that we will drift and wander so that he can defeat us through temptation.

So, it is important to walk with God. The Bible declares in Psalm 37:23,

> *"The steps of a good man are ordered by the LORD: and he delighteth in his way."*

If God is ordering our footsteps, then we are emphatically sure not to wander. Stay with God. Keep up with His plan for your life. As long as He is close, you will be ready for the devil when he brings temptation your way. Do not allow yourself to wander.

STEP III

LET THE DEVIL AND HIS TEMPTATION FLEE FROM YOU

"...and he will flee from you." James 4:7

Chapter Eleven

Close Out Your Sin Account

"Wherefore come out from among them, and be ye separate, saith the Lord, and touch not the unclean thing; and I will receive you,"
II Corinthians 6:17

As we enter this new section, we are going to deal with the principles of separation. In other words, how to drive a wedge between the old man, his cravings and lusts, and the new man who embraces the spiritual things of God. As we look at separation, we understand that the scripture says we should be separated—from the old ways, desires, activitics and actions. In order to separate yourself from the old things, you must effectively close out your sin account.

If you do not close out your sin account, then the enemy will always have access to you. He will always wreak havoc on your plans and rain on your parade. The enemy has been a joint account holder. When you participated in sin, he was there and had access to your mind and your thoughts. This makes it necessary to bring closure to the places he had access to. The devil, in the past, has made a deposit in your account. When he makes a deposit, he leaves it there for future use. He will bring it back to you when he feels that it is needed to keep you in bondage, to keep you incarcerated and to keep you outside of God's kingdom.

When the devil is getting ready to do something in your life or thinks that you are getting too close to God, he will take a spiritual ATM card and make a transaction. This is why it is necessary to close out everything the enemy has on us. It is often difficult for us to go forward if we continue to live in the past. The scripture says in II Corinthians 5:17,

> *"Therefore if any man be in Christ, he is a new creature: old things are passed away; behold, all things are become new."*

The enemy brings temptation through old doors, which deal with our lusts, insecurities and fears from our past. If you used to drink, then expect him to tempt you in the area of drinking. If you used to do drugs or run women, expect him to come in a similar fashion. If it worked back then, the devil believes it will work again.

If you are going to be successful, you must learn to close out old business. In Philippians 3:13, Paul says,

> *"Brethren, I count not myself to have apprehended: but this one thing I do, forgetting those things which are behind, and reaching forth unto those things which are before,"*

This simply means that closure is being brought to the old life. This does not mean that you totally forget where you came from. It means that it is no longer a part of you. If it is a part of you, then the devil will always have access. He will always come through the dark corridors of your intrinsic being to connect you to your past. But, Jesus said, whom the Son sets free, "…ye shall be free indeed."[20]

The Gospel according to St. John, Chapter 8, tells the story of

[20] St. John 8:36 If the Son therefore shall make you free, ye shall be free indeed.

a woman that was caught in the act of adultery. The men of the temple and some religious potentates brought her to Jesus Christ. They told Jesus that according to the law of Moses, the woman should be stoned and asked Him what should be done. Jesus spoke and said, "...He that is without sin among you, let him first cast a stone at her."[21] Jesus again stooped down and wrote on the ground. The woman's accusers were convicted by what they heard and departed one by one. When Jesus stood up again and not seeing any of the men asked, "Woman, where are those thine accusers? Hath no man condemned thee?" The woman answered, "No man, Lord." And Jesus answered, "Neither do I condemn thee. Go, and sin no more."

This is significant because if she was ever going to be free of her past and all that it entailed, it was necessary for her to make a break from her activities, her mind set and everything she had been a part of. She had to start a new life in Christ. This is what we must do as Christians.

It is important for us to recognize that if the devil is going to flee from us, then we have to set an atmosphere that he is not comfortable with. If you are holy and spiritual, then it causes the devil and his demonic forces to want to separate from you. Throughout the scriptures, God admonishes us to live a clean and holy life. This is not just to get us ready for heaven, but also helps us close the door on temptation and sin. It helps us change our destination from hell to heaven. God wants us to not only help ourselves, but to help each other in our endeavors to separate ourselves from sin and falling prey to temptation.

Galatians 6:1 says,

> *"Brethren, if a man be overtaken in a fault, ye which are spiritual, restore such an one in the spirit of meekness;*

[21] St. John 8:7 So when they continued asking him, he lifted up himself, and said unto them, He that is without sin among you, let him first cast a stone at her.

considering thyself, lest thou also be tempted."

God gives us the responsibility to help others close out their accounts in order to stabilize us in our walk with Christ. God wants us to be separated from our past, through Him and His Will. He wants us to close out our past and open up our future. The Lord is looking for people of integrity that will stand on His promises; that when temptation does arrive, the enemy will not be able to infiltrate because all of the places of access have been sealed off. If there has ever been a time to sever past things, it is now. It is time to make a change. It is time to embrace our future. You can only walk towards your future when you have agreed to leave your past.

Chapter Twelve

Let the Devil Go

"He that committeth sin is of the devil; for the devil sinneth from the beginning. For this purpose the Son of God was manifested, that he might destroy the works of the devil." I John 3:8

It is time to let the devil go. The scripture says,

> *"Submit yourselves therefore to God. Resist the devil, and he will flee from you."* James 4:7

If you have done your job in terms of submitting yourself to God and putting up a strong resistance, there is no reason why the devil will not flee from you. The problem may not be that he will not go, but it may be that you will not let him go.

Many times there are multiple factors involved in getting victory over temptation. It seems that the enemy has an around the clock operation working for him to defeat us. This is true in a sense because he certainly throws everything at us, but sometimes it is not the devil that defeats us. It is something that you have done or left undone that forfeits the victory that you are supposed to obtain. Because of your own infractions and malfeasances, you tend to lack the spiritual endurance to be victorious during your times of temptation. In essence, you are giving the enemy a foothold to set up camp on your territory and to defeat you. Ephesians 4:27 tells us,

> *"Neither give place to the devil."*

When you allow the enemy to have a spot on the campground or a piece of real estate to work on, then you are yielding a place that would normally contain spiritual power. It is your responsibility to release all ties from your past transgressions and clean up your spiritual environment so that God can saturate every aspect of your being.

Letting the devil go simply means you are trusting God to use His power to put the devil at bay. It means that you trust His process. If you have submitted yourself to God and put up a strong resistance against the devil then he will have to exit. Letting the devil go speaks to a total disconnection that you have from him. It deals with your severing your ungodly relationships, activities, mindsets and lusts. It is releasing him and divorcing yourself from him. There is nothing in you that wants what he has. It is serving the enemy an eviction notice, and setting all of his belongings outside of your house. As we embrace God and solidify our relationship with Him, we in turn sever all ties with the devil. We are taking action to be free in God and loose from every bondage of the enemy. There is nothing he can do for us because we belong to God now.

> *"He that committeth sin is of the devil; for the devil sinneth from the beginning. For this purpose the Son of God was manifested, that he might destroy the works of the devil.* 9 *Whosoever is born of God doth not commit sin; for his seed remaineth in him: and he cannot sin, because he is born of God."* I John 3:8-9

Chapter Thirteen

Redirect Your Misplaced Passions

"For when we were in the flesh, the motions of sins, which were by the law, did work in our members to bring forth fruit unto death.
6 *But now we are delivered from the law, that being dead wherein we were held; that we should serve in newness of spirit, and not in the oldness of the letter."* Romans 7:5-6

Throughout this book we have dealt with the many aspects and challenges of strong temptation. The main objective, as stated earlier, is to lay out the process to overcome temptation by using biblical principles and instructions. It is necessary to examine the copious facets of temptation in order to effectively defeat it when it arrives. One of the areas that I believe requires attention is the vacuum and residual aftermath that temptation leaves when it is finally gone.

When we are tempted, a tremendous amount of energy and focus is required to deal with that particular temptation. Everything that you have going on in your life is temporarily placed on hold and the necessary effort is put forth to address the situation at hand. Your time, attention and mind are sequestered "center stage" of this concentrated focal point. When the time of testing is over, even though you may be successful, there is still an array of ideas, feelings and afterthoughts that must be confronted and effectively re-routed.

If these thoughts and emotions are not ministered to, they can lead to frustration, depression, bitterness or worse, an invitation to "re-run" the same temptation. Do not allow the devil to get an "absentee victory." Even our Lord Jesus Christ, after He was tempted by the devil, had a period of time in which He was ministered to. St. Matthew 4:11 states,

> *"Then the devil leaveth him, and, behold, angels came and ministered unto him."*

It is important to redirect your misplaced passions. I believe that victory over temptation is really not consummated until the passion connected to the desire of that temptation has been effectively and conclusively redirected. Do not misunderstand me. I believe that you should celebrate your triumph over the enemy as long as you understand that you must deal with the "fall out" that comes along with it. By not taking action, you may experience devastating consequences.

Have you ever seen anyone put up a strong resistance and actually overcome a situation—maybe crack cocaine or alcohol? They were doing really well and their victory was not a fluke. After a whole month, they were still going strong and they used to do it every day, but the next time you see them, they have relapsed. What happened? They were dealing with a "void" that they were not prepared for. All of a sudden, the passions, energies and desires were left hanging like live electric wires. It was alright for a while, but they soon needed to be reconnected and redirected.

Redirecting your misplaced passion is a positive thing. I try to live my life like everything is coming from God. If God allows temptation in a particular area, then He must mean for me not just to resist it, but also to address it. My thought is that maybe God is trying to show me areas that I am or could be potentially weak in. If something has "tempted" me, then there must be some latent passion

He wants me to address. An introspective look is in order.

How Do I Redirect My Passions?

As we seek to understand what to do with our misguided passions, it is important for us to examine our overall purpose, our reason for being on Earth. I believe if God gives you certain passions that are engrained in your personality (do not get passion confused with lust), then the manifold wisdom of God has designed a place for each of them. Everything that God "fearfully and wonderfully" created in you fits somewhere.

Moses had a passion for the Children of Israel; so much so that he killed an Egyptian man.[22] Later, God took that same passion and used it as Moses led the Children of Israel out of the bondage of Egypt. Before the Apostle Paul used his passion to establish and guide the new Christian Church and to write a great portion of the New Testament, his passion was used to persecute the church and the Christians.[23] Great things can happen when passions are redirected.

So What Should I Do with My Passions?

From these examples and other scriptural passages, the Bible seems to indicate that we should direct our passions into spiritual devotions and ministry work. In the 5th Chapter of James, the writer concludes a didactic discourse of Christian mannerisms by telling us to direct our passion to prayer. James 5:16-17 states,

> *"Confess your faults one to another and pray one for another, that ye may be healed. The effectual fervent prayer of a righteous man availeth much.* 17 *Elias was a man subject to like passions as we are, and he prayed earnestly…"* [Emphasis added]

[22] Exodus 2:11-12 And it came to pass in those days, when Moses was grown, that he went out unto his brethren, and looked on their burdens: and he spied an Egyptian smiting an Hebrew, one of his brethren. 12 And he looked this way and that way, and when he saw that there was no man, he slew the Egyptian, and hid him in the sand.

[23] Acts 22:4 And I persecuted this way unto the death, binding and delivering into prisons both men and women.

The Word of God also speaks about placing our energies, emotions and enthusiasm in the work of the ministry. Our Lord Jesus taught a parable in St. Luke, Chapter 19, about a nobleman who was leaving the country for a period of time and the responsibility that he gave to his servants. The story centered around their activities in the absence of their Lord and warned against the dangers of idleness.

> *"And he called his ten servants, and delivered them ten pounds, and said unto them, Occupy till I come."*
> St. Luke 19:13

This word "occupy" does not just mean "take up space", but take your energies and talents and employ yourself in an occupation. Ecclesiastes 10:18 states,

> *"By much slothfulness the building decayeth; and through idleness of the hands the house droppeth through."*

This is what happens when our passions lie dormant. There are other warnings about not focusing your passions into the work of the ministry. In II Thessalonians 3:11 Paul addresses a group in the church where he states,

> *"For we hear that there are some which walk among you disorderly, <u>working not at all</u>, but are busybodies,"*
> [Emphasis added]

Likewise, I Timothy 5:13 addresses some of the women in the church,

> *"And withal they learn to be idle, wandering about from house to house; and not only idle, but tattlers also and busybodies, speaking things which they ought not."*

In conclusion, I believe that God wants you to redirect your passions into something or some area that is going to build up the Kingdom of God. Ephesians 4:1-3 says,

> *"...walk worthy of the vocation wherewith ye are called.*
> 2 *With all lowliness and meekness, with longsuffering, forbearing one another in love;* 3 *Endeavouring to keep the unity of the Spirit in the bond of peace."*

And II Peter 1:10 says,

> *"Wherefore the rather, brethren, give diligence to make your calling and election sure: for if ye do these things, ye shall never fall..."*

Chapter Fourteen

See Your Victory Through

"For whatsoever is born of God overcometh the world: and this is the victory that overcometh the world, even our faith." I John 5:4

Do you know there is nothing that can stop you from reaching your destiny? There is really no one that can block your blessing. God has literally placed before you a spiritual open door.[24] If you miss out, it will only be because you hindered yourself. A temptation is just that—a temptation. It is not a sin to be tempted. The very word implies that you can triumph over it. It does not have to ruin your life. If you make the right choice and decide not to take the bait, then you will be successful.

Success, however, only comes by enduring through the entire "time" of testing. Each temptation is like taking the S.A.T. It is not just one test, but a battery of tests. When Jesus was tempted of the devil in St. Matthew, Chapter 4, He was tested in three different areas. Understand that you must continue to submit to God and resist the devil through the balance of your temptation. Please realize that getting a few questions right does not mean that you have aced the test and even passing one test does not mean that you have passed the entire examination series. It is necessary to see your victory through. II Timothy 2:3 states,

[24] Revelations 3:8 I know thy works: behold, I have set before thee an open door, and no man can shut it: for thou hast a little strength, and hast kept my word, and hast not denied my name.

"Thou therefore endure hardness, as a good soldier of Jesus Christ."

A good soldier fights harder when the fighting gets fierce. He "digs in" and fortifies himself against the strongholds of the enemy. He is strictly obedient to the orders that he has been given. Psalm 37:23-24 says,

"The steps of a good man are ordered by the LORD; and he delighteth in his way. 24 *Though he fall, he shall not be utterly cast down: for the LORD upholdeth him with his hand."*

A good soldier sees his victory through. If you are going to pass, then you have got to last! Keep doing your best to fulfill God's Will. Keep the faith and believe that God is working it out. Continue to walk upright before the Lord and soon your trials will become your testimonies. Psalm 84:11 tells us,

"No good thing will he withhold from them that walk uprightly."

In the heat of temptation continue to hold out. Your good will pay off. You will not only be blessed with the joys of defeating your temptation, but also with a resident strength that comes from the experience of successfully enduring. God teaches us how to overcome through the process of doing good. Listen to Romans 12:21,

"Be not overcome of evil, but overcome evil with good."

Doing "good" means following God's lead. If you are going to be an overcomer, you must be mindful not to abort your efforts to resist too quickly. Before you celebrate, ensure that the temptation is actually over.

Overcoming may entail what may seem to be an endless and arduous process of going through, while keeping the standards of God's Word. This requires patience and faith until the victory comes to pass. Maintaining your praise and worship will help to keep your spiritual equilibrium. See your victory through!

EPILOGUE

Shut The Door Behind You

"And Jesus said unto him, No man, having put his hand to the plough, and looking back, is fit for the Kingdom of God."
St. Luke 9:62

Those that plow always look forward. It is essential that if you are going to be a true overcomer, you must embrace the things on the horizon. This simply means that everything that God has for you to do is in front of you. Therefore, what has passed is in the past. This does not mean that you cannot learn from your past, however, you cannot live in it. On the contrary, I believe your past was meant to help you deal with the future. Certain tools and wisdom are ascertained from your experiences.

You must learn how to effectively "shut the door" behind you. The greatest enticement of your temptation is going to be linked to something from your past. The devil deals with your deep history of sin to try to resurrect the "old man." In St. Luke 17:32, Jesus Himself warns us to,

"Remember Lot's wife."

The 19th Chapter of Genesis reveals the tragic story of this young woman. She could not get to her future because she could not leave her past. Her life and death are a memorial of what happens when you do not shut the door behind you. She was out of Sodom, but Sodom was not out of her.

You do not have to be bound by your past and you do not have to live in fear of temptation. If you are in Christ, God has granted you a brand new citizenship with the privileges of being free and victorious. II Corinthians 5:17 states,

> *"Therefore if any man be in Christ, he is a new creature: old things are passed away; behold, all things are become new."*

Being a new creation in Christ gives you the power to let the "old things pass away." This means that you can get your deliverance in the area that you are struggling in, defeat recurring problems and shut the door behind you. Victory is available for you if you are willing to bring closure to your situation.

> *"Looking unto Jesus the author and finisher of our faith; who for the joy that was set before him endured the cross, despising the shame, and is set down at the right hand of God."* Hebrews 12:2

Keep looking forward, keep looking up and shut the door behind you.

Scriptural References

James 5:7
II Timothy 3:1-5
James 1:1-2
Psalm 40:2
James 4:7
St. John 8:32
St. John 14:6
I Corinthians 10:13
Hebrews 4:15
St. Matthew 16:24
St. Matthew, Chapter 4
II Chronicles 30:8
St. Luke 10:19
Acts 3:19
I John 1:9-10
St. Matthew 5:6
St. Matthew 26:39
I Peter 5:6
Psalm 46:1
Philippians 2:5
Genesis 3:3-4
Proverbs 23:7
James 1:8
St. Matthew 4:4
St. Matthew 4:7
St. Matthew 4:10
Psalm 119:105
Revelations 3:10
I John 2:5
I Peter 5:8
Hebrews 4:12
I Timothy 6:6
II Timothy 3:5
II Corinthians 6:14
Acts 2:42
Philippians 4:8
Ephesians 6:16
St. John 1:14-16
Ephesians 4:27
Ephesians 4:22
St. Mark 14:38
Genesis 4:7
Hebrews 12:1
St. Mark 14:38
Genesis, Chapter 19
Proverbs 13:15
Proverbs 13:6
Philippians 3:3
St. Matthew 26:41
Romans 7:18
Ephesians 6:10-12
I Corinthians 9:27
II Corinthians 10:3-4
Romans 8:3
II Peter 1:4
James 1:14
Ephesians 6:12
Ephesians 6:13-17
Isaiah 54:17
I Timothy 6:12
St. John 14:26
I Thessalonians 5:6-8
Ephesians 5:15
Psalm 37:23
II Corinthians 5:17
Philippians 3:13
St. John 8:36
Galatians 6:1
St. John 8:7
I John 3:8
Romans 7:5
St. Matthew 4:11
Exodus 2:11-12
Acts 22:4
James 5:16-18
St. Luke 19:13
II Thessalonians 3:11
I Timothy 5:13
Ephesians 4:1-3
II Peter 1:10
I John 5:4
Revelations 3:8
II Timothy 2:3
Psalm 37:33
Psalm 84:11
Romans 12:21
St. Luke 9:62
St. Luke 17:32
Hebrews 12:2

About Pastor Lyle Dukes and Co-Pastor Deborah Dukes and Harvest Life Changers Church, International

Pastor and Co-Pastor Dukes have been commissioned by God to reach the world and change lives through the preaching and teaching of God's Word. It is their desire to see every believer broken free from the chains of bondage and walking progressively in the manifestation of God's promises.

Over the past seven years, Harvest has become a life-changing place of growth and deliverance through the power of Jesus Christ. God has continued to send souls to hear these anointed and appointed vessels. Today, the church has over two thousand members and countless visitors who come to worship God, be saved, delivered and set free.

If you are ever in the Woodbridge, Virginia area, we invite you to worship with us on Sundays at 8:00 a.m., 9:00 a.m. and 11:30 a.m. and on Wednesdays for Pastoral Bible Teaching at 7:30 p.m.

For additional information, you may call (877) 867-3853 or visit www.harvestlifechangers.com.